D0493483

"Righteous ire, directed at very deserving tar[...]
are shot through with a moral umbrage an[...]
Logan, The Guardian)

"Funny, angry and tightly written....McGonagall combines anger, polish
and carefully crafted verse in a way which recalls John Cooper Clarke....
If the word 'poetry' is putting you off, get over it." (Susan Mansfield, The
Scotsman)

"Brilliantly anarchic, verbally agile, always a treat." (Joan Bakewell)

"Rampaging through the vicissitudes of modern life with stanzas like
Panzers." (Phill Jupitus)

"The poetry of Elvis McGonagall is a world steeped in the darkest humour,
peaty whisky and joy and I love it – it is the profound humanity beneath
the punchlines that melts my heart." (Salena Godden)

"I couldn't imagine the poetry scene without Elvis McGonagall. His verse
is wonderful – full of chippy invective and scorching satire. My favourite
Elvis, just ahead of Costello." (Luke Wright)

"A cluster of gems from the deliciously acid 'Gimme Some Truthiness'and
the tender 'Miracle' to the succinct, brutal 'The Johnsons'. Elvis tears a
hole in the backside of today." (Mik Artistik)

"A deep-fried ball of disillusioned bile stuffed into a tartan jacket
and thrust on stage, Elvis McGonagall has us laughing through the
tears as the ship sinks. Good hair, too." (Jonny Fluffypunk)

"Bitingly satirical, irreverent, intelligent and laugh-out-loud funny, Elvis
McGonagall has deservedly earned a reputation as one of UK performance
poetry's most cherished stars." (Nathan Filer)

"Funnier than most stand-ups, wittier than most wits, Elvis resides in
zeitgeist, always passionately pushing the envelope. A class act."
(Hardeep Singh Kohli)

"Like a mini William Wallace of words giving the ruling political class the
middle satirical finger Elvis puts the Bang into Bang Said The Gun every
time he stands on our stage." (Dan Cockrill & Martin Galton, Bang Said
The Gun)

"Ebullient, intelligent and deeply amusing sociopolitical satire."
(Murray Lachlan Young)

Stand-up poet, comedian and broadcaster, armchair revolutionary and walking shortbread tin Elvis McGonagall resides at the Graceland Caravan Park somewhere in the back of beyond, where he scribbles satirical verse while drinking malt whisky and listening to Johnny Cash.

Two series of his sitcom *Elvis McGonagall Takes a Look on the Bright Side* have been broadcast on BBC Radio 4, where he appears regularly as well as popping up occasionally on the telly.

Elvis is the 2006 World Slam champion, the compère of the Blue Suede Sporran Club and performs at literary and music festivals, comedy and cabaret clubs, pubs and dodgy dives up and down the country and abroad.

Elvis also gigs with his band The Resurrectors, 'an unholy marriage of whisky-soaked, radical, stand-up poetry and Caledonian punkabilly rock 'n' roll'. The band's debut album *Gie' It Laldy!* was released on Bar-Ox Records in 2018.

A deftly witty wordsmith, sharp and subversive but not afraid to be plain daft, Elvis has been spitting his scabrous diatribes against the powers that be since 2003. And look at the state of the world now. So that's seventeen years of futile ranting.

A live recording of his show *One Man and His Doggerel* is available on Laughing Stock Records and a collection of his poems from 2003 to 2017 entitled *Viva Loch Lomond!* was published by Burning Eye Books in 2017. With this new volume Elvis McGonagall's meteoric rise to glittering showbiz obscurity continues apace.

Elvis McGonagall: destined perhaps to remain a complete and utter cult, but huge in North Korea.

elvismcgonagall.co.uk

Tony Kerins fills sketchbooks with drawings of the very ordinary – cars in streets, clouds in the sky and people all over the place. It's good training for illustrators, especially when the text is as rich and witty as this one. And he should know, because, with forty years experience behind him, he's just written a book about it, *Walking and Drawing with Tony Kerins*.

tonykerins.com

ELVIS McGONAGALL

complete & utter cult!

Poems 2017-2020

Illustrated by Tony Kerins

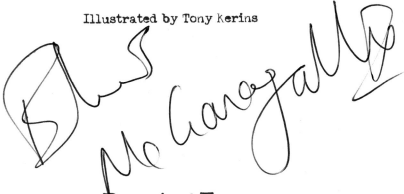

Burning Eye

BurningEyeBooks
Never Knowingly
Mainstream

Copyright © 2020 Richard Smith www.elvismcgonagall.co.uk
Illustrations © 2020 Tony Kerins www.tonykerins.com
Cover photograph by Andrew Lee @PhotographyAndrewLee

The author asserts the moral right under the Copyright, Designs and
Patents Act 1988 to be identified as the author of this work.

All rights reserved. No part of this publication may be reproduced,
stored in a retrieval system, or transmitted, in any form or by any
means without the prior written consent of the author, nor be other-
wise circulated in any form of binding or cover other than that in
which it is published and without a similar condition being imposed
on the subsequent purchaser.

This edition published by Burning Eye Books 2020
www.burningeye.co.uk

@burningeyebooks

Burning Eye Books
15 West Hill, Portishead, BS20 6LG

ISBN 978-1-911570-95-0

"Don't sweep away the shards of your shattered dreams. Buy superglue and stick them back together"*

*From 'The Thoughts of Chairman Wow', wordslinger in chief for The People's Republic of Groove.

for Jean Smith (1934-2018)

The Author

CONTENTS

THE POWER OF LUST

Written for BBC Radio 4 Archive on 4's 'A Brief History of Lust'.

The roses had no thorns in Eden
The milk and honey flowed at no cost
Then lust slithered in with forbidden fruit
One bite and paradise was lost

Don't blame it on Eve, the girl couldn't help it
Blame the wiring in her prefrontal cortex
We're all in thrall to the flesh machine
History is cast in desire's swirling vortex

King Henry couldn't keep it in his codpiece
Herod dribbled drool at Salome's wiggle
Lust is sated, heads decapitated
Wars declared for a bit of slap and tickle

Ample cleavages can topple empires
Bondage and whips can launch a thousand ships
Lust-breathed Antony let Rome in Tiber melt
To straddle Cleopatra's curvy hips

Lust is a bunga-bunga bacchanal
Lust lives in palace, bordello and slum
Presidents' trousers are caught around their ankles
Popes, potentates and peasants all succumb

Monsieur Hollande's blonde said, 'Keep your helmet on'
Pizza-delivery-playboy fashion
Mr Major made Currie red-hot, 'Oh yes'
Then tucked his shirt back in his pants of passion

But lust just doesn't stop at triple-X sex
It's not only Raquel Welch in *Bedazzled*
Lust hungers for Iggy Pop's liquor and drugs
Lust devours, lust is on the razzle

Lust dusts itself in golden glittering bling
A gilded scaffold for a queen's execution
Fifty-two Fabergé eggs, diamonds and pearls
Pave the road to bloody revolution

Lust craves control of the great unwashed
Lust is a power trip on testosterone
Lust debases and debauches, lust depraves
Lust can turn a bunch of tulips to stone

Lust insists you *can* always get what you want
Lust says what is yours is mine, all mine
Lust must overtake the Joneses, come what may
Lust inclines towards the philistine

Lust is a sticky-fingered, drunken glutton
Lust loves to grope, grab, plunder and gazump
Lust is a domineering sugar daddy
Lust has the Tango-tanned* face of Donald Trump

The cistern of our lust will never be filled
Lust will blindly snatch, steal and spend
Lust forever needs the latest shiny apple
One bite too many and this world will end

* Or maybe 'Irn-Bru face' is a more appropriate carbonated drink
metaphor as I'm afraid he is technically half-Scottish. Apologies on
behalf of Scotland, everyone. Given his sclerotic complexion and the fact
that 50% of his genes have a proclivity for fried food, surely to God a
cardiac arrest is imminent?

9.3% SWING

Written shortly after the 2017 general election.

A red island in the sea of Cotswold blue*
A red outcrop in these blue remembered hills
We're not 25-grand smug shepherds' huts
We're red brick, spit and sawdust, woollen mills

A red rose amidst the snarling thorns of May
A red flag sewn from Stroudwater Scarlet
We're not the headmistress's blue-rinse smile
We're the crimson kiss of a wanton harlot

We're not Farrow & Ball 'complacent blue tit'
We're not weekend waxed jacket and tweed knickers
We're not honey-dipped, chocolate-box bollocks
We're not mimsy-boo boutique more-tea-vicars

We're anarchist printers, poets and painters
We're the ghosts of Huguenot weavers
We sing protest songs up a hornbeam tree
We're the New Lawn vegan-green believers**

We're not Johnnie Boden, we're Jonny Fluffypunk
We wield pen and brush, not polo mallet
We steer to the left through canals of Budding beer
A splash of vermilion from art's rich palette

We don't twitch the curtains of seething disapproval
A Little Metropolis, we think out loud
Welcome mat unfurled, we're citizens of the world
We're the People's Republic of Stroud

* In 2016, having spent fourteen years living in a wee village in Dorset, we decided it was time to leave our godforsaken rural idyll. To be honest I was going a bit King Lear, raging at the wind and rain and the tourists and the endless packs of Lycra-clad Bradley Wiggins wannabes careering through the village as if it was their own private velodrome. And so we moved from the countryside to the Cotswolds. Which does sound a bit counterintuitive. The Cotswolds are a strange place, the kind of place where rock stars retire to make 'award-winning artisan cheese'.

The floppy-haired bloke from Blur makes a cheese called 'Little Wallop', which is a 'totally unique goat's cheese wrapped seductively in a vine leaf'. It retails at £7.95 for 140g from a shop called Pong. That's about fifty quid a kilo. You've got to be one fucking successful ploughman to have that in your lunchbox. But that's the Cotswolds for you, a land of showbiz farmers and £25,000 luxury shepherds' huts. Not that there's any shepherds in those huts. Oh no. Who's in the hut? Why, it's the feckless numpty who called a referendum on the EU, Fat Dave. Possibly dressed as a shepherdess like Marie Antoinette at Versailles, busy shovelling the floppy-haired bloke from Blur's exorbitant cheese into his chubby cheeks and hiding from Danny Dyer.

However, we moved to Stroud, which is different from the rest of the Cotswolds. A thriving cloth town during the Industrial Revolution, it's full of old mills and canals and has a proud history of counterculture and radical protest. On election night in May 2017 the map of south-west England was a sea of blue with one wee Jackson Pollock splat of red – ooh! that's us! Labour have taken back the seat – we're the People's Republic of Stroud!

** We have a carbon-neutral, vegan football club up the road. 'Here for the salad! You're only here for the salad!' we'd sing at the opposing fans if we could, but we can't because we're too weak and undernourished. We are so alternative it hurts. Up to a point, because a) one of those old mills is now a Waitrose, a convenient two-minute walk from where we live and b) the Tories regained the seat at the December 2019 election. Our new MP thinks Stroud is a 'bouncy town'. God help us.

For more on the joys of Waitrose turn to 'Papa's Got a Brand New Bag'.

GIMME SOME TRUTHINESS

Written for BBC Radio 4 Archive on 4's 'A Brief History of Truth'.
'Truthiness' is a term coined by the American satirist Stephen Colbert
to describe the idea of passion, emotion and certainty over information.

We're sick and tired of unvarnished verity*
Two plus two is five if said with sincerity
Ignorance is strength, wealth is austerity
All we want is truthiness

Soundbite-clickbait-fakey-breaky news
University-of-Google YouTube views
Cock-and-bull-soft-soap-snakeoil-schmooze
Give us this day our daily truthiness

Porky pie Boris – you've got to have a laugh
Populist politics – snigger 'n' snarf
Praise Lord Gove and pass the polygraph
It's just a bit of banter – truthiness

Big red Brexit bus full of cream crackers
350 million smackers?
Sell us bent bananas, kick proof in the knackers
Take back control of truthiness

The world needs a leader whose pants are on fire
A Dorito-toad-faced Twitter Town crier
Tweet tweet tweeting atop his golden spire
Give us all some Trumpiness**

Evidence is dull, gut feeling suffices
Barack Hussein Obama founded ISIS!
Mexican Muslim massacre crisis!
Truthiness – Trump it up!

Down the rabbit hole with Alice, tumble 'n' spin
To win is to lose and to lose is to win
Corbyn is victorious, he's in like Flynn***
It's emotional, this truthiness

Through the looking glass, reality's an act
Justin Bieber's labradoodle's phone was hacked
Even if it didn't happen it's still a fact
In-your-Facebook truthiness

We only know what we believe in our mind's eye
Don't diss the opinions of the vox populi
I always tell the truth even when I lie
And that is God's honest gospel truthiness

* We live in an era of utter bullshit, the age of 'alternative facts' and 'fake news' – i.e. lies.

** Donald Trump. The unexpected item in the bagging area. The saveloy in your vegan BBQ. The elk with dysentery in the Jacuzzi of life.

*** Jeremy Corbyn. Ostensibly a decent, serious, principled chap surprisingly thrust centre stage. But not at all decent to some. Oh no. 'He's dangerous. A dangerous Marxist nihilist.' Really? How many nihilists make their own jam? 'OK, then,' the naysayers say, 'he's a communist. That's Bolshevik bramble jelly he's making. He's got a little Lenin hat and his cat's called Chairman Miaow. I saw him at Waterloo station buying a ticket to Salisbury. He had a plastic carrier bag full of organic Novichok. He grows it on his allotment, you know. He rides around that allotment on a Shetland pony in his M&S vest and pants. He's the Poundland Putin.'

'Oh no he's not!' shout his fans. 'Look at his initials! JC! He's the Messiah, sent to feed the 5,000 with his jam. Jam yesterday, jam tomorrow and now, for the first time, jam today! Raspberry jam for the many, not rose petal and prosecco preserve for the few! Jam, jam, jam, jam, jam! (Don't mention Jerusalem.)'

Sadly for Jeremy he didn't get into number ten, but I fully expect him to appear on 'Dragons' Den' any minute now, turning his culinary hobby into a commercial enterprise. He could be the new Reggae Reggae Sauce – 'Jezza Jezza Jam' – although the world of glitterati groceries is a cut-throat business. For every success story there's a dozen abject failures. I mean, you've got your Paul Newman salad dressings, your Loyd Grossman peshwari naan bread and the daddy of them all, Barry Norman's pickled onions, but who remembers Mariella Frostrup's fondant fancies now, eh? Sunk without trace. Whither Adrian Chiles' chipolatas? Kim Kardashian's non-clumping cat litter? Are any of these real? Who knows? Who cares? It's a post-truth world, baby; anything goes.

THE IMMIGRATION ALPHABET

A is for Alien. A 'foreigner'. A scary 'foreigner'. Bursting into our country like the thing erupting through John Hurt's rib cage in that film. Be afraid. Be very afraid.

B is for Blame. Don't blame it on sunshine, moonlight or good times. Or even the boogie. Blame it on the 'bloody migrants'. Coming over here with their beards. Suspicious beards. Beards full of hummus.

C is for Calais – engraved on the broken hearts of exhausted Syrians and frightened Sudanese, the bereaved of Afghanistan, the ruined of Iraq. Refugees fleeing torture, terror and war. Wars we started.

D is for DNA. The DNA of 'Cheddar Man', the first modern Briton, 8,000 years BC. Black skin. Blue eyes. Take back control, Cheddar Man. Take back control of your country.

E is for Economic migrants. Not you, José, in your Armani cashmere coat, scowling on the touchline. You are 'Premier League'. You are an 'expatriate'. Come on in, the salary's lovely. 'Economic migrant' means you, Souleyman from Senegal, hiding in that lorry. You are not financially viable. Goodbye.

F is for Farage. Fearmonger-in-chief. The floating jobbie in the toilet bowl of public life that may never be flushed away.

G is for Ghetto. A ghetto full of exiled minorities. Poor wee Russian oligarchs and Saudi princelings forced to subsist in the joyless penthouse luxury of Knightsbridge.

H is for Hostile. A hostile environment for illegal aliens. 'Oi! ET! Fuck off back to Mars, you little green bastard benefits cheat!'

I is for Indian. 'Let's go for an Indian. I feel like chicken jalfrezi tonight!' Well, you can't have it because the Taj Mahal's chef can't get a work permit and has been deported back to Bangladesh.

J is for Jews – forced by law to wear a patch of yellow cloth. In England. In the year 1275.

K is for Kent – a former English county now annexed to the Middle East after its capture by an invading force of half a dozen men in a rubber dinghy.

L is for Language. 'Hasta la vista mamma mia achtung zut alors!' Funny foreign, double Dutch, all Greek to me. English is the lingua franca round here. Not fucking Italian, Pedro.

M is for Marks. Michael Marks of Marks & Spencer, Polish-Belarusian immigrant and purveyor of fine British underpants. And Karl Marx. German immigrant and inventor of the hipster beard.

N is for No. No room. 'Am I alone in feeling Britain is full?' tweeted zany multi-millionaire novelty act and professional beard strimmer Noel Edmonds. 'You are not alone Noel,' tweeted multi-millionaire business dick Duncan Bannatyne from his home in Portugal.

O is for Oh. As in 'OMG, Priti Patel is Home Secretary'. Priti Patel, the daughter of Ugandan-Indian immigrants, who is 'ending free movement to open Britain up to the world'. Sweet baby Jesus Christ almighty.*

P is for Passport Control. Bloated, global, gold-fingered plutocrats, just waltz on through the fast-track lane. All you impoverished, homeless, hungry outcasts stand over there in that long, long, long, long queue.

Q is for the Queen of England, descendant of Albert of Saxe-Coburg and Gotha's German princely house of Wettin and of the Danish royal house of Schleswig-Holstein-Sonderburg-Glücksburg, and married to Prince Philip of Greece and Denmark. Rule Britannia!

R is for the Roots of reggae, rocksteady, ska, natty dread, drum 'n' bass, dubstep and grime stowed away in the hold of the Empire Windrush as it set sail from Kingston, Jamaica, in 1948, bound for Tilbury docks. Bringing the rhythm to England's two left feet.

S is for Swarm. A 'swarm' of migrants. A deluge, a flood, a tidal wave, a tsunami swamping our green and pleasant land. A plague of sticky-winged locusts stripping the fruit from our trees for the minimum wage.

T is for Tesco, founded by the son of Jewish migrants from Poland. The original 'Polski sklep'. Every little zloty helps. Na zdrowie!

U is for UKIP. The UK Indignation Party. Shaking their fists and shouting at the British muezzin in his minaret.

V is for Vessels packed to the gunwales with the desperate displaced. Human cargo careening 'cross the Med in floating coffins.

W is for Wombles. A multiracial underground community of undocumented asylum seekers from Bulgaria, France, Venezuela, Siberia, Japan and the Isle of Mull who pick up dog shit and empty crisp packets in a public park because the indigenous population can't be arsed. Respect due, Orinoco.

X is for Xenophobia, which is a fear of minimalist Japanese interior design.

Y is for You. And you. And you. And you. And me. And him. And her. And them. And us. All of us. Outsiders, incomers, strangers. Climb up your family tree, take in the view. If we look back far enough we all come from somewhere else, from Ashby-de-la-Zouch to Xanadu.

Z is for Robert Zimmerman, whose chimes of freedom flash for the abandoned refugee. So ring out, majestic bells, ring out those chimes of freedom from this land. Because everyone deserves to reach a safe harbour. Everyone needs somewhere to belong.

* Priti Patel has appointed a 'Clandestine Channel Threat Commander' whose primary responsibility is to make the Channel route 'unviable for small boat crossings'. A bit redundant. Farage is already on the cliffs of Dover with his binoculars day and night like a tragic, overgrown Boy Scout trying to earn his Racist Activity Badge.

HELLBOUND

Written as a song for my band The Resurrectors. Yes, a band. Look at me and my mid-life crisis. Actually, I've just done the maths... mid-life is optimistic. Anyway, this is a cheery, toe-tapping, slam dance in the mosh pit number about the imminent apocalypse. If only I'd included a reference to a highly infectious disease caused by a severe acute respiratory syndrome coronavirus this could have been a prophetic, chart-topping hit.

We're staring into tiny mirrors
We're all shouting at the same time
We're angry wasps trapped in a glass
We're starring in our own pantomime

The clowns are running the circus
The village idiots are in town
The beast is slouching to Bethlehem
Sticky fingers clutching his crown

Nero's tuning up his fiddle
The fat lady's clearing her throat
Orla Guerin's at the city gates
The Good Samaritan's getting his coat

We're all hellbound for Satan's sweatshop
Down, down, down in the bottomless pit
Let's go on the randan* – drink and dance
Tomorrow's long gone – this is it

Forsaken souls are capsizing
The promised land is out of reach
We're drowning in seven seas of plastic
Dead mermaids are littering the beach

The grapes are withering on the vine
The old green fuse has lost its lust
The Tower of Babel's burning
Ashes to ashes, dust to dust

Cloven hooves are clattering
The stench of brimstone's in the air
Lucifer's stamping on the angels' harps
His red-hot poker's up their derrières

17

We're all hellbound for Satan's sweatshop
Down, down, down in the bottomless pit
Let's go on the randan – drink and dance
Tomorrow's long gone – this is it

Jesus Christ is taking selfies
God's crying in his beer, blind drunk
Philistine fools are rattling their jewels
The next shiny thing's already defunct

The wine is turning to vinegar
Bono's face is on the Turin shroud
The sun is blistering black as crow
Noah's hammering nails into clouds

It's raining fear, it's raining loathing
Arabian nights are thick with drones
The petrol pumps are full of blood
The desert is a carpet of bones

We're all hellbound for Satan's sweatshop
Down, down, down in the bottomless pit
Let's go on the randan – drink and dance
Tomorrow's long gone – this is it

There's Nazis in chinos and loafers
Dress-down Friday fascists on the rise
They're pouring paraffin on bonfires
Goose-stepping with the Lord of the Flies

The car is heading for the clifftop
Dick Dastardly is at the wheel
Muttley's sniggering in the back
This cartoon is on its final reel

The well's run dry of milk and honey
The rascal multitude ain't got a crust
Bells are ringing out a silent peal
The wheels of time have turned to rust

We're all hellbound for Satan's sweatshop
Down, down, down in the bottomless pit
Let's go on the randan – drink and dance
Tomorrow's long gone – this is it**

* 'On the randan': a night out on the bevvy.

** The human race is going backwards. We peaked on 10th January 2016, the day that David Bowie died. That's just a coincidence. There are people out there who believe that Bowie was the glue that held the universe together. That's a fanciful notion. We all know, don't we, dear readers, that Ronnie Corbett was the glue that held the universe together, and now Ronnie's gone the good ship lollipop is sailing down the shitter. Anyway, if you'd like a soundtrack to the end of days then do head over to Bandcamp and download our album 'Gie' It Laldy!'

GHOST TOWERS IN THE SKY

Stash your cash in London's glittering attic
Have filthy lucre laundered 'n' tumbled dry
Get a safe deposit box that's pragmatic –
A penthouse in a ghost tower in the sky

Reach new heights of luxury, redefine place
Invest in a vertical Versailles
Beyond the ordinary, ultra-prime space
A silent, empty ghost tower in the sky

Soar amid the City's glacial façade
The cloud-capp'd erections thrust up on high
Cheesegrater, Gherkin, Shiny Dildo Shard
Viagra Towers, tumescent in the sky

Make capital gain your personal domain
Procure a buy-to-leave global pied-à-terre
Own the finest lifestyle money can obtain
Breathe in your own exclusive, private air

En-suite helipad carpeted in silk
Hanging gardens flown in from Babylon
Infinity pool of perfumed asses' milk
Marble ballroom with a pop-up Elton John

Dramatic views of regeneration
Dynamic growth driving out the obsolete
Survey the vibrant urban aspiration
Pret a Manger *literally* at your feet!

Embrace gilded postcode quality control
Silver bulletproof gated surveillance
Paranoid dogs with diamond teeth on patrol
Protect your asset from unwashed assailants

Overlook cardboard beds on streets of gold
Sidestep the big issue, turn a blind eye
Shut the door on the down-and-out in the cold
Stay cloistered in your ghost tower in the sky

That massive middle finger to poverty
Priapic palace for prince and potentate
Pity poor developers of property
Building El Dorado next to sink estates

Insulate opulence from the worn and drab
Paper over cracks in council tower blocks
Transform the low-income, high-rise concrete slab
Into a plastic-wrapped trap, a tinderbox

One flame can fuel 500 burning beds
A twenty-four-storey crematorium
A charnel house of horror, seventy-two dead
Burning Grenfell hell in memoriam

Jutting out heavenward, a black, rotten tooth
Aching monument to England's decay
Clad the poor in contempt, deregulate truth
Choose complacent disregard, come what may

Plumb uncharted depths of wanton neglect
Manage steep decline with impropriety
Outsource responsibility and respect
Tear apart the fabric of society

Demolish the library and the jazz club
Bulldoze the hospital and school, gentrify
Knock down the corner shop, Odeon and pub
Stick up another needless ghost tower in the sky

Which some day will be ruins, shadow and dust
The Temple of Mammon's sarcophagi
A graveyard of greed, base metal turned to rust
As a distant generation wonders why

Why did we let racketeers frame the rules?
Why were we taken in by their artifice?
Who let them build alabaster vestibules?
What kind of dick lived in a house like this?

This land is a common treasury for all
Not a fiefdom for the few to occupy
No more gated citadel fences and walls
We need homes, not ghost towers in the sky

A MIRACLE
(FOR HELEN)

I have witnessed a miracle.

This miracle does not involve loaves, fishes, bread, wine
or raising the dead from their cold, stony grave.

It does not feature walking on water, parting the Red Sea
or a virgin birth.

This miracle is not a member of Smokey Robinson's
backing band.

It did not take place on 34th Street.

It did not take place at Celtic Park, Glasgow on 17th May
2014 when St Johnstone beat Dundee Utd 2-0 to win the
Scottish Cup (although that did actually happen. I was
there. Row A, Seat 30, Jock Stein Lower Stand).

It is not the result of a wish upon a shower of shooting
stars falling from the spangled sky like diamond petals
from the flowers of the gods.

The miracle is the fact that I found you.

Of all the billions of souls wandering this lonely planet,
I found you.

Of all the gin joints in all the world, you walked into a bar
where I was drinking on a hot, humid night in Hong Kong.

And now, twenty-eight years later, this miracle still happens
every day.

Just an everyday miracle.

A cup of tea in bed.

An evening on a sofa watching *Spiral* with two cats and
a bottle of wine, wood burning in the stove, shouting
'Engrenages!' in unison as the opening credits roll.

A four-hour round trip to Southampton for a poetry gig on Valentine's Day – with a stop at Membury services to eat cold falafels in the pissing rain, because you're concerned that's far too far for one person to drive.

Yes, I found you. You found me. We found each other.

And you still put up with me. And that is a miracle.

The miracle of love.*

* The one thing that matters in this sometimes sorry world. This poem is the property of Helen (Mrs Elvis) and she'd like it known that she's given her permission for it to be included here. I was giving this piece a heartfelt rendition at WOMAD with Helen in the audience when, unbeknownst to me, a wasp lurking at the top of her can of cider stung her on the lip, which then swelled up to such an extent it crossed her mind that these might be the last words she heard as she expired from anaphylactic shock. Fortunately she survived.

STATING THE BLEEDING OBVIOUS

The sky is blue, the grass is green
All that glitters is not gold
Snow is white, water is wet
The Pope is Catholic, ice is cold

The sea is salty, birds have wings
Tock follows tick follows tock
Grizzly bears shit in the woods
Piers Morgan is a massive cock*

* I've always thought that this assessment was perfectly fair - nay, self-evident - but this poem has been ruined by COVID-19. At one point Piers Morgan seemed to be the only journalist calling out our 'government' for their shambolic handling of the crisis. He has not been acting like a massive cock of late. Still a cock, but not a massive one. Accordingly, please feel free to substitute Piers with anyone else you think deserving of the epithet 'massive cock', e.g. Tim Whatsisname, the Wetherspoons Twat. Further evidence of Piers' rehabilitation came with the news that Donald Trump had unfollowed him on Twitter. This should have been celebrated were it not for the fact that it's one of the signs of the end of days described in the Book of Revelation.

#MENOTYOU

A piece concerning the pernicious effects of the patriarchy. I should point out for the sake of clarity that my day job involves flouncing across clifftops in a fedora, ocelot coat and Cuban heels declaiming lovelorn verse in a fey manner and thus I am clearly not the narrator here. In much the same way that John Lennon was not the walrus. Or indeed the egg man.

I do this one with the band. Performed through a megaphone in a bass growl à la Tom Waits.

I am Tarzan beat of hairy chest
I am macho Marlon Brando vest

I am suited, booted silverback
I am potent aphrodisiac

I am dollar bills and pheromone
I am cigar smoke and cologne

I am 'Arrogance' by Hugo Boss
Frankly, my dear, I don't give a toss

I am alpha male, king of kings
You are women, my playthings

I am mover, I am shaker
I am your career maker

I am Big Enchilada
Without me you are nada

I am your fame, your success
I know you know that no means yes

I call the shots, I run the show
I'm entitled to fellatio

I am titan, I am mogul
I am sleaze, I am ogle

I am raging bull 'n' rutting ram
I am wham-bam-thank-you-ma'am

You say victim, I say slag
I am stallion, I am stag

I am toxic salamander
I am phallus, therefore I philander

I am cock and balls, I am knob
I am girth and heft and throb

I am locker-room-jockstrap hard
My beefsteak brings all the girls to the yard*

And they're like, it's bigger than his
Damn right it's bigger than his

Look at it! Look! Look at my dong!
Look at my dick, my rod, my schlong!

Taste my charisma, touch my power
Massage my manhood, see me shower

I am crusty paw and swagger pants
I am the silence of my sycophants

I am pussy-grabby grope up skirt
You say predator, I say flirt

I am fluffy hotel bathrobes
Let me feel your Golden Globes

Watch me wank, I am vulgarian
I am Onan the Barbarian

I am braggadocio
You are slut, my quid pro quo

I am testosterone, I am sweat
I am 300 pounds of threat

I am bourbon breath in your ear
I am your shame, I am your fear

* A reference to the 2003 R&B hit 'Milkshake' by Kelis and the only
faintly amusing line in this piece. My 2018 Edinburgh Fringe show 'Full
Tartan Jacket' was billed as comedy. There were some baffled faces in the
audience when I performed this.

I am brute force without escape
I say begging for it, you cry rape

I am liberal, I am Woke
Don't laugh at me, I am no joke

I am Harvey, I am Bill
I am Kevin, Donald, Louis, Phil

I am vengeance, I am paranoia
I am impunity, call my lawyer

I am misogyny incarnate
My crimes swept under thick red carpets

I am everyday abuse
I am flaccid, limp excuse

No one told me you are equals
I am endless sordid sequels

I have demons that must be fought
I'm so sorry, sorry I've been caught

I am your misinterpretation
I am my rehabilitation

I can't help it, I am sick
I am unrepentant prick

I am the dregs of a bitter cup
Surely to God my time is up?

Surely to God my time is up?

Surely to God my time is up?

TAKING BACK CONTROL

Blighty's taking back control of Christmas
He's dreaming of a Christmas that is white
A Christmas free from filthy foreign snow
A ho-ho-wholly Great British silent night

A Victorian yuletide frozen in time
A bleak midwinter that never, ever thaws
Singing, 'Arrivederci, panettone!
And fuck off back to Lapland, Santa Claus!'

Blighty's burning his Norwegian Christmas tree
The brandy in his butter ain't French, mon frère
He's returning his turkey to Istanbul
He's sticking Brussels sprouts up his derrière

A-wassailing he will go in the workhouse
With consumptive cherubim and seraphim
He will feast upon yesterday's cold parsnips
Pass the roasted seagull, Tiny Tim

All he wants is to pull his own cracker
He does not want your Christmas bratwurst, Herr Schmidt
But I want Spanish chestnuts and hygge*
I want a Dukla Prague away kit**

So I will fill my face full of stollen
Get Brahms and Liszt on glühwein, dance and yell
'Buon Natale y Feliz Navidad!
Fröhliche Weihnachten et Joyeux Noel!'

* Wikipedia describes 'hygge' as 'a Danish and Norwegian word for a mood of cosiness and comfortable conviviality with feelings of wellness and contentment'. Don't know if it's compulsory to wear a Fair-Isle-style jumper à la Sarah Lund in 'The Killing' while enjoying a bit of hygge. Anyway, it's certainly preferable to the word 'Brexit'.
Jesus wept. I'm sick of it. Sick of its pointless stupidity. 'I've painted my shepherd's hut a lovely shade of Soft Brexit - it's from the Farrow & Ball Spurious Nostalgia range.'

Apparently Brexit is 'the will of the British people'. The British people couldn't be trusted to name a fucking ship. 'You can't have Boaty McBoatface,' they say, but you can unravel the Gordian knot that is forty years of peaceful cooperation and legislation on a whim because a cabal of fanatical shysters, amoral spivs and vaudeville vandals have persuaded you that the EU is an ersatz piñata and if you thwack it hard enough all the toys and sweeties will fall out for you boys and girls. And so off we float into the Atlantic on our own. The MP John Redwood insists that Brexit means that we'll now be "controlling our own fish". Sounds like a pitch for a new TV reality game show. This country is fucked. That might sound a bit dramatic and I might be accused of hyperbole, but I know that there'll be no Brittany butter with sea-salt crystals available in Waitrose come the 1st of January 2021. Yes, that bad. But on the other hand there'll be aisle upon aisle of chlorinated chicken and Krispy Kreme doughnuts. Praise the Lord and pass the ammunition.

** It's important to have at least one Half Man Half Biscuit reference in any poetry collection.

29

ME, MYSELFIE AND I

This is a 'found poem': every line (except one) is extracted from a broadsheet Sunday supplement magazine article about 'wellness' in which a few of its aficionados shared their typical days with us (I admit that I may have reordered these words for my own nefarious purposes in a kind of 'lift and twist'). This type of article appears every January when the human race feels compelled to make resolutions to improve itself and discover its potential because it's a new year. My advice would be 'don't bother'. The cold, grey, bleak, miserable, windswept tundra of a month that is January is not the time to try to become a holier-than-thou suburban Dalai Lama. The only thing worse than January is February, and come February 1st you'll be back to pouring vodka on your deep-fried raspberry Pop-Tarts for breakfast, weeping bitter tears of self-loathing at your lack of self-discipline. If you're going to try anything, try hibernating. Anyway, there are people out there who subscribe to this wholly healthy, holistic hype all year round. They don't just live their lives; that's too prosaic. They 'curate their own lifestyle experience'.

5.55am
I wake up having had seven hours and forty-one minutes' sleep. I know this is the perfect amount for me
The first thing I do is scrape my tongue using a copper tongue scraper to get rid of toxins
I turn on the near-infrared light at the end of my bed and sit there for seven minutes meditating
I take a shot of probiotics and Quinton Isotonic, a supplement that comes from plankton
I then do online yoga for twenty minutes and stare at the sun – I use the Pomodoro Technique

6.50am
I leave the flat and fist-bump the concierge
I've fist-bumped him every morning for four years
I go to F45 training*, an intense fitness regime
The community at F45 is incredible
I like to mix with like-minded people
I'm not going to hang out with people who like to drink a lot at the pub
I then go for a dip in the Serpentine – it's horrible

7.45am
I come home, fist-bump the concierge and have a glass of Rebel Kitchen raw coconut water
I fill out a spreadsheet on my computer inputting my weight, my urine pH, my hydration and how well I've slept
I turn on my HumanCharger, a device that shines light into my ear to give me energy
I have a cold shower for 90 seconds
I make a delicious smoothie with 7.8g of protein in it

8.15am
I start work. I'm freelance. I work by my Himalayan salt lamp
It helps absorb the magnetic and radioactive waves from wifi
Goodness knows what they could be doing to my body
I wear blue-light-blocking glasses that cut out junk light
I don't drink coffee
I drink a litre of water a day – either San Pellegrino or Love Hemp
Water which I buy from Planet Organic
I haven't drunk tap water for two years
I've been teetotal for seven months
Alcohol makes my tongue really dry, which I hate
If I go out I'll always take a bag of nuts and fist-bump the concierge
If I have a meeting I may go for a walk with the person I am meeting
– Steve Jobs used to do this
Between meetings I'll try to have a shot of activated charcoal – they
sell it at Pret now. We're so blessed in Britain

1.30pm
I go out for lunch at the same time every day
I fist-bump the concierge
I follow a high-fat, low-carb, mainly ketogenic diet
My body has 7.5 per cent fat
I eat lean meat but I do feel really bad for the animals
I don't eat any processed food at all
I eat pudding like everyone else

3.00pm
I switch on my Himalayan rock salt lamp

6.30pm
I finish work, fist-bump the concierge, then walk to the gym
The Tube is filthy and not good for your health
I then go to the clinic I founded in Mayfair and have an hour of
hyperbaric oxygen
On Saturdays I follow up with a magnesium and amino acids
intravenous drip treatment

8.00pm
I don't eat dinner

* I tried Pilates once. Pontius Pilates. Quite a niche exercise regime.
Uncomfortable and time consuming, takes about three days. Good for the
lats though.

31

8.30pm
As soon as I get back to my flat I fist-bump the concierge and lie on a bed of nails

10.00pm
I feed my mind by reading for 10–40 minutes

10.40pm
I watch an episode of something that adds value to my life or a *Breaking Bad*-type drama
I only watch half the episode, no more. We only live once

11.10pm
My orange night-time light activates on my phone to allow my body to start shutting down

11.45pm
I switch on my Himalayan rock salt lamp
I then get into bed. I use an earthing bedsheet
I have natural bedding and pillows so I'm not inhaling petrochemicals all night
I lie down and close my eyes
I aim to get seven hours and forty-one minutes' sleep
If I don't get enough, everything falls apart

2.00am
I'm not sure that the concierge likes me very much

CLOUD CUCKOO LAND

The mercury's rising, who cares why?
Cock a deaf ear, turn a blind eye
Crank up the thermostat, let's all fry
Cloud Cuckoo Land is burning

The tide is high and getting higher
The forecast's famine, flood and fire
Take a spin in your tumble dryer
Cloud Cuckoo Land's perspiring

It's scorchio eight days a week
Motherwell's hotter than Mozambique
Ride your jet ski up shit creek
Cloud Cuckoo Land is your land

Grow your own dollars, crisp and green
Fight wars to feed your limousine
Wake up and smell the gasoline
Cloud Cuckoo Land is burning

Defrost Antarctica, let it sink
Watch the Amazon jungle shrink
Log in to Amazon.com, Inc.
Cloud Cuckoo Land delivers

Wash your hair in *Perrier*
Buy more junk, then throw it away
Obsolescence is here to stay
Cloud Cuckoo Land is wasteland

Build airports where the buffalo roam
Chainsaw down an orangutan's home
Drown in an ocean of *Styrofoam*
Cloud Cuckoo Land is burning

Factory farm the fatted calf
Harpoon a whale, garotte a giraffe
Write Mother Nature's epitaph
It's a laugh, Cloud Cuckoo Land

Spray paraquat on a honey bee
Climb a Siberian coconut tree
Cook all the fish in the boiling sea
Cloud Cuckoo Land is melting

Ignore the firmament's expanse
Be chop-chop busy-busy human ants
A pestilence in underpants
Cloud Cuckoo Land is burning

Choke the skies, air mile after mile
Swim with polar bears down the Nile
Fill your trolley in the excess aisle
Cloud Cuckoo Land's all-consuming

Heat your patio in freezing June
Fly your avocados from the moon
Use your leaf blower in a typhoon
Cloud Cuckoo Land's convenient

Incinerate science, facts are dead
Wrap a roll of cling film round your head
Frack planet Earth, try Mars instead
Cloud Cuckoo Land is burning

The future's gone; it's when, not if
Oblivion beckons in a jiff
Follow your satnav off the cliff
Cloud Cuckoo Land is falling

Yet when humanity's run its race
Still this blue marble will spin in place
As plastic bags drift on through space
And Cloud Cuckoo Land has vanished into dust*

* Turns out that rampant consumption is despoiling the planet. Who'd have
thunk it? Any minute now you're going to see a polar bear floating down
your high street on a melting iceberg. And that polar bear will be angry.
He wants to buy some underpants. And socks. But Matalan have shut another
branch and it's all boarded up. And don't even think about telling the
polar bear to socially distance.

(THE RESISTIBLE RISE OF) THE MILKSHAKE MARTYR

Another one written for the band. Imagine a dissonant, Chas-'n'-Dave-style knees-up. The spring of 2019 saw a vogue for dousing far-right thugs and purveyors of gutter politics with high-sugar dairy products. Banana and salted caramel flavour in the case of Nigel Farage.

Splattered in thick, white, creamy stigmata
Here he comes – it's the Milkshake Martyr

He's a bully beef bloke, proper Dunkirk
A bitter drinker with an ashtray smirk

He's down your boozer charging his glass
He's slapping your back and the barmaid's arse

Cracking bawdy jokes from the good old days
Bemoaning Blighty's effeminate malaise

Salt of the earth, an ordinary chap
He's got a cheeky *Peaky Blinders* cap

British pork in his little chipolata
Don't you cry for the Milkshake Martyr

The world's his lobster, he's paid top dollar
His overcoat's got a velvet collar

He's selling second-hand pride door to door
Pride straight as an arrow from Agincourt

He's flogging Dr Freedom's magic pills
Manufactured in dark satanic mills

He's offering you the moon on a stick
Union Jack socks on, he's a maverick

Nice chunk of cheddar on his ciabatta
Don't you cry for the Milkshake Martyr

Where there's no hope, opportunism knocks
He's squeezing himself through your letterbox

He's creeping upstairs in your carpet slippers
He's in your kitchen grilling your kippers

Feet up with a fag, watching the snooker
He's knocking back your duty-free sambuca

You're his best PayPal, he's your Facebook friend
Ignorance and fear are the perfect blend

A pair of pickled eggs in his frittata
Don't you cry for the Milkshake Martyr

He's curdling the custard on your crumble
Dressing up in khaki, ready to rumble

He's bouncing on next door's trampoline
He's pissing on their lawn, he's venting his spleen

He's locking your neighbour in her garden shed
Mrs Khan's hijab's filling him with dread

He's screaming 'Traitor!' at your French bulldog
'Woeuf, wouef!' He hates its foreign dialogue

Red hissy-fit face like a burst tomato
Don't you cry for the Milkshake Martyr

He's giving you a job licking his brogues
You're meeting his mates, they're loveable rogues

He's clearing your streets of human bric-a-brac
He's sticking his bollards up your cul-de-sac

He's bricking you up, he's fencing you in
Keeping out strangers with the wrong colour skin

Singing, 'Two world wars and one World Cup!'
Chocks away, Biggles, keep your pecker up

Aniseed balls in his piñata
Don't you cry for the Milkshake Martyr

He's dropping his trousers in front of Fritz
He's having a laugh, he's puttin' on the Blitz

He's tearing down eco-vegan rainbow flags
He's taking England back, from riches to rags

He's telling you everything's hunky-dory
Let the people eat knickerbocker glory

No swastikas, no silly moustaches
Don't mention the F-word – f-f-f-fascist

Bag of nuts and a pint of Magna Carta
You've been had by the Milkshake Martyr

THE JOHNSONS

Linton Kwesi Johnson: dub poet
Robert Johnson: red-hot Delta blues
Samuel Johnson: lexicographer
Michael Johnson: Mr Golden Shoes
Magic Johnson: wham bam ma'am slam dunk
Amy Johnson: the queen of the air
Don Johnson: Ray-Ban Armani cop
Wilko Johnson: machine-gun guitar glare
Ben Jonson: Renaissance dramatist
Ulrika Jonsson: Swedish weather front
Holly Johnson: the voice of Frankie
Boris Johnson: shameless cunt*

* If you're offended by the use of robust Anglo-Saxon language, I should
point out that a) the two most offensive words in the piece are 'Boris' and
'Johnson' and/or b) you can try replacing 'shameless cunt' with 'improbus
cunnus' to spare your blushes, 'cause you can say anything in Latin, can't
you? The Auld Etonian celebrity 'character' politicians love a bit of it.
  However, in the interests of balance, let's have another go at this from
a different angle:

BORISH

Thanks to Andrew Wood (see 'Word Up') for this word.

Boris Spassky: chess grandmaster
Boris Yeltsin: fond of a vodka or two
Boris Berezovsky: Russian oligarch
Boris the Spider: a song by the Who
Boris Karloff: Frankenstein's monster
Boris Becker: serve, volley, grunt
Boris Pasternak: Doctor Zhivago man
Boris Johnson: shameless cunt*

* Oh dear - same ending. Sorry. A pity, because he's so much more than this, isn't he? Have a look at 'Please Leave Our Town'.

THE UNCO GUID, TRUE BELIEVERS

A wee nod to all the Rabbie Burns fans out there with this title. This is
another one written for the band - hence the chorus. As yet unrecorded
thanks to the pandemic.

Our truth is best, it's fundamental
Our vision is the only view
Our severity is gentle
What we believe is good for you

Our rectitude is on parade
Our virtue is a sacred cow
Every day is a moral crusade
We're so much holier than thou

Our leader has been heaven-sent
To turn back time and plough the sand
Don't question us, do not dissent
We're on our way to the promised land

Join in the chorus, sing our song
We know we're right 'cause you're all wrong

Blind faith demands deep devotion
Doubting Thomases are traitors
We are intransigence in motion
We walk up down escalators

We're sorry we don't apologise
We'll never dismount our high horse
No ifs, no buts, no compromise
You can't have ketchup *and* brown sauce

We will not bend, we will not budge
Our thoughts are bound by discipline
Purists like us were born to judge
We can dance on the head of a pin

Join in the chorus, sing our song
We know we're right 'cause you're all wrong

We're seriously serious
Our laughter is mechanical
Our decency's imperious
Sackcloth on, get puritanical

Consensus reigns in our dominion
We're shouting in an echo chamber
We can't forgive a wrong opinion
We're shouting in an echo chamber

Behold our wholly humble halos
Our sainthood burns with Day-Glo zeal
We've got more followers than J-Lo
Check out our righteous sect appeal

Join in the chorus, sing our song
We know we're right 'cause you're all wrong*

*   There's a lot of shouting out there, but not much listening going on.
Social media is like a cross between the mediaeval stocks and a circle
jerk. 'Compromise' is a dirty word. Everything's polarised; there's no room
for nuance or debate in public discourse. Ideological purity is demanded.

PLEASE LEAVE OUR TOWN

During a 'Prime Ministerial' walkabout in Morley, a local resident gently asked Boris Johnson to 'please leave my town'.

There's no sunlight in these uplands
There's a Tupperware lid on the sky
Our rose-tinted glasses are tarnished
Hope's eternal spring has run dry

There's a sleeping bag by Starbucks' door
There's a robbery at the food bank
There's a queue outside the hospital gates
There's a hearse in the taxi rank

Now you roll up with your trademark shtick*
The glib, sniggering schoolboy gags
The crikey, crumbs, golly-gosh bluster
The trail of bullshit, the humblebrags

The tailor-made Worzel Gummidge look
The Charge of the Light Brigade British spunk
The spaff-it-up-the-wall rehearsed pratfall
The let-them-eat-cake Etonian punk

Pack up your circus, cardboard clown
On your tiny bike, please leave our town

You are whoopee cushion farting out lies
Plastic flower squirting Sophocles
Naked ambition sheathed in a codpiece
Drunken uncle on the flying trapeze

Buller, Buller bully in a china shop
You are smashed crockery and broken glass
You are blundering imperial goat fuck
Slapdash dog-ate-my-homework farce

You are Brexit Island car boot sale
You are flog England off by the dollar
You are cash in a pole dancer's G-string
You are private profit, public squalor

You are up your own arse with a ladder
You are Fozzie Bear with a machete
You are Fat Andy Warhol cabaret act
Mr Jolly Bollocks, barking yeti

Pack up your circus, cardboard clown
On your tiny bike, please leave our town

We are hemp-smelling, nose-ring crusty
We are sentimental victim Scouse
We are blubbing, tank-topped bum boy
We are chicken-frit big girl's blouse

We are French turd EU traitor
We are flag-waving picaninny
We are tribal watermelon smile
Cannibal Papua New Guinea

We are ridiculous letterbox burqa
We are Islingtonian herbivore
We are Nazanin Zaghari-Ratcliffe
We are dead Libyan body eyesore

We will not buy seats for your panto
We will not utter your cartoon name
If you are the punchline, the joke's on us
We are all just pawns in your game

Pack up your circus, cardboard clown
On your tiny bike, please leave our town

---

* Boris Johnson. A man with the carefully cultivated demeanour of a scary, drunken children's entertainer. A man who hid in a freezer to avoid being interviewed by Piers Morgan. A man whose favourite song must surely be Boney M's 'Hooray! Hooray! It's a Holi-Holiday'. A man who, despite being a self-serving charlatan and carpetbagger, now resides at No. 10 Downing Street and 'leads' a 'government' filled with rank mediocrity and destructive, laissez-faire zealots like Michael Gove. You can't get rid of Gove, can you? He's like a dogshit-smeared boomerang you never wanted. And there's something called a 'Rees-Mogg'. What the fuck is that? Something PG Wodehouse has left in the back of his fridge for too long?

43

WELCOME TO OUR TOWN

For God's sake, don't pick this book up and read this poem at random
before you've looked at the previous one and think, 'Ooh! A right-wing
poet - how novel!' Mrs Elvis pointed out to me that some people out there
actually like Boris Johnson and we have to try to understand his appeal
to effectively counter it. So I wrote this as a companion piece to 'Please
Leave Our Town'. A kind of Jekyll versus Hyde thing. An interesting
exercise. I still think he's a shameless cunt.

These uplands are drenched in sunlight
The sky is an ocean of blue
There's gold at the end of the rainbow
Each halcyon dawn dazzles anew

There's a Caffè Nero next to Starbucks
There's a craft gin bar in the old bank
There's a queue for the farmers' market
There's an Uber in the taxi rank

Now you drop by with your trademark charm
The funny gaffe and irreverent gag
The endearing golly-gosh fluster
The little-white-lie scallywag

The dishevelled man of the people
The Great British spunk-filled naughty boy
The off-the-cuff spontaneous stunt
The unadulterated real McCoy

Tell us a joke, bring the house down
Come on in, welcome to our town

You are trumpet-tongued nil desperandum
Walking thesaurus talking Sophocles
You are planet-brained Rolodex mind
You are genius madcap wheeze

You are bulldozer of balderdash
You are boisterous breath of fresh air
You are victory, vim and vigour
You are totes hilarious hair

You are Great British yellow brick road
You are can-do bet your bottom dollar
You are pole dancer for British business
You are save us all from Marxist squalor

You are unleashed British irony
Latin sprinkled like clever confetti
You are star-dusted Tory Elvis
You are great, big, jolly, blonde yeti

Tell us a joke, bring the house down
Come on in, welcome to our town

We hate hemp-smelling, nose-ring crusty
We scorn sentimental victim Scouse
We laugh at blubbing, tank-topped bum boy
We mock chicken-frit big girl's blouse

We curse French turd EU traitor
We fear flag-waving picaninny
We dread tribal watermelon smile
Cannibal Papua New Guinea

We ridicule letterbox burqa
We loathe Islingtonian herbivore
Who is Nazanin Zaghari-Ratcliffe?
Why is the Middle East such a bore?

We are dress circle, front row fanboy
We are standing ovation for your fame
Boris, Boris, Boris, Boris, Boris
Boris is the name of the game

Tell us a joke, bring the house down
Come on in, welcome to our town

WORD UP

Written for the Stroud-based artist Andrew Wood's Word project. This piece uses the words - in bold - that Andrew has displayed outside his studio in the style of the Hollywood sign: andrew-wood.com/the-word

In **Dyslexia dog is God**
You can **live** on **love and peas**
Sing **Happy New Ear, Alan** akbar!
Watch the **polite** catch **moist** thieves

You can dwell in the Backache **Motel**
Park in its multi-storey **farage**
Rent a semi-detached council **horse**
Vote for that **duck** Nigel **Garage**

Run a **mole**, ride a **house**, walk the **plimsole** line
Take some antithe**presents** – don't jump
If you're blue they're **Putin** on the Ritz
That's why the lady is a **Trump**

Trump is **love police** and **fuck the earth**
Trump is **scrotum heart**ed **nostril proud**
Trump is **suck** my **trouser donkey**
Trump will **never ever** be very **Stroud**

Stroud is **Noah** when it's stormy
Stroud is **Sairam Allah**, be our guest
Stroud is a **woman** called **Polly***
Stroud is **why not? Stroud** is **yes**

* Polly Higgins, author of 'Eradicating Ecocide'.

47

PAPA'S GOT A BRAND NEW BAG

PART 1

The wee man in the flat cap and anorak
who trundles down the hill to Waitrose* each day
now scampers along helter-skelter
breezily swinging his brand new bag.
His brand new eco-friendly shopping bag
emblazoned with the words 'Parsnips & Sprouts'.
I wonder why the wee man chose this bag.
Does he only buy root veg and brassica?
Nothing but British root veg and brassica –
not for him funny foreign groceries.
Just down-to-earth produce from English soil –
no plantains, polenta or papaya,
although his bag was made in India,
four thousand, five hundred miles away.
It's a 'bag for life' and 'BPA free'
as well as being 'suitable for vegans'
and at £4.50 it's cheaper than
the ten-quid Heston from Waitrose bag
that features an otter in fisherman's clothes
or a toad eating chips in a deckchair.
A squirrel playing golf's another option
or an Edwardian sea-bathing donkey.
But the wee man's no fan of Blumenthal's bags,
he likes a bag that simply states what it holds.
Other bags were for sale in his preferred range.
He could have chosen 'Chocolate and Chilli',
singing, 'Arriba! Yo soy Mexicano!'
as he cha-cha-chas to the checkout
with jalapenos, tacos and tortilla,
a crate of tequila his Aztec gold.
Or he could have plumped for 'Blue Cheese & Pear' –
entre la poire et le fromage, ooh la la,
basket oozing with cave-aged Roquefort,
a tarte tatin or two for a taste of France.
Or how about 'Pancakes & Blueberries'?
Yelling, 'God bless American snacks, yee-haw!'
as he rides his trolley like a cowboy
full of fat-fried peanut butter Twinkies.
He steered well clear of 'Ice Cream & Sprinkles',
the words suggesting something quite unseemly
involving Donald Trump in Bacofoil pants
in the penthouse suite of a Russian hotel.

Me? I would buy the 'Goats Cheese & Honey' bag,
dreaming of salty, sun-kissed Greek tavernas,
craving taramasalata and feta,
breathing in the piney tang of retsina.
I'd hear the clunk and jangle of the goat bells
in the whitewashed village olive groves,
the lonely mountain chapel a distant speck
from my hammock underneath a cypress tree.
But I've already got a bag – so I don't,
and I don't buy the bag that says 'Bacon & Eggs'
or 'Turmeric & Milk' or 'Quinoa & Kale'
or 'Pomegranate Molasses & Miso'.
I enter Waitrose with my Morrisons bag
in a vain attempt to disguise the fact
I'm now a bourgeois hypocrite class traitor
and I know I'm not fooling anyone.

---

*   The first time I visited our local Waitrose I was like Crocodile
Dundee in New York – agog at the cornucopia of delights on offer.
Himalayan pink salt! Artisan artichoke puree! At last! The essentials of
life! Sun-dried porcini powder! It was all too much. I was used to the
Co-op in Wareham, where the shelf-stacker was a master in the art of Zen
minimalism. Look! A can of baked beans! For you!
Then I got all J Alfred Prufrock angsty about it. Do I dare shop at
Waitrose? Do I dare buy an organic peach? Fuck it, I thought – yes! There's
free coffee in there! In you go, son!
However, it wasn't long before they changed the rules. No longer could
you waltz in, wave your wee loyalty card and get a free coffee. No. You
now had to buy something. Excluding tobacco. Excluding lottery tickets.
Possibly excluding super-strength cider, for all I know. In any event it
seemed to me that there was a subtext to this rule change – i.e. this shop's
not for you, McGonagall, it's for Mungo and Jocasta from Painswick. You
get yourself down to the pound shops in the Merrywalks shopping centre
(and if you've never been to Stroud I should point out that 'Merrywalks'
is nominative determinism gone very badly wrong indeed).
And I realised that the rule change was a metaphor for our divided
nation. It's still all about the haves and the have-nots, isn't it? And we
know who the haves are, don't we, dear readers? They're the people who use
the word 'winter' as a verb. When they order a drink at the bar they say
'I'll have'. No pleasantries. They're entitled to that drink. And it's the same
with power. They're entitled to it and, once they've got it, they cling on
to it. We'll only get it back when we pry it from their cold, dead hands.

PART 2

I enter Waitrose with a short shopping list –
toilet rolls, tinned tomatoes, pasta, soap –
but what was once a cathedral of plenty
is now a braying tweed *Supermarket Sweep*.**
It's all gone Hieronymus Bosch in there,
a hellscape of Duchy Organic panic.
Anguished cries rend the air – 'There's no fresh ginger!' –
as the moleskin-trousered locusts strip the shelves,
four forlorn globe artichokes left to wither
in the barren, fruitless fresh produce aisle.
I leave with a bottle of Metaxa,
cat food, crisps and reduced-price hot cross buns,
thinking, *Now that's what I call stockpiling*.
You can keep your penne all'arrabbiata
and your soft, clean, unchafed Andrex arses;
I'm ready for bloody moon, fiery flood and plague,
I say to the nonplussed security guard
as I emerge into a very different world.

** At least March's panic buying will have been good training for the
2021 Brexit food riots.

50

WHAT A STATE!*

Parade Mr Churchill's Victory V
Play 'Colonel Bogey' on your kazoo
Britannia's unchained from slavery
Oompa-loompa-doopity-do

Free at last, as free as Mr Humphries
Free from the yoke of je ne sais quoi
Free from continental patisserie
Carte blanche to be who we really are

A local island for local people
The Full English, Manuel, por favor
The cliffs of Dover will always be white
Mind your language and shut that door

Last bastion of proper prejudice
Mustn't grumble, form an orderly queue
Twitch Hyacinth Bucket's net curtains
Innit marvellous, you silly old moo?

Land of sun-dappled, verdant hedge fund
Of rose-clad Airbnb stately homes
Aspidistras and antimacassars
Angry seagull shit on garden gnomes

Of gravy-stained pomp and circumstance
Pantries full of Rudyard Kipling's cakes
Never mind the quality, feel the width
Ooh, Matron! We're oh so Hattie Jacques

Roast beef faced boys in mustard corduroys
Quaff foaming ale served by buxom wenches
Winsome milkmaids skip o'er rolling hills
Jaunty ploughmen do lunch in the trenches

Miss Marple cycles to Wetherspoons
Through autumn mist and winter hail
A wicker man burns on the village green
As the air raid sirens gently wail

Cry, 'God save Mrs Slocombe's pussy'
Have a nice cup of tea and a bicker
Pass the royal wedding biscuit tin
You are awful, but I like you, vicar

Shoulders back, lovely boy, don't panic
A stiff upper lip is essential
Show the world there's lead in your pencil
As we unleash Britain's potential

We'll boldly go back to the future
To the good old days and beyond
In splendid isolation from strangers
They don't like it up 'em, Mr Bond

Last gasp – ramp it up – whatever it takes
Get it done on a wing and a prayer
With lionhearted bulldog spirit
Gin-soaked regret and quiet despair

So sing, Lofty, sing, sing some Vera Lynn
As we fight pestilence from overseas
We'll take it on the chin, Gunga Din
No room here for foreign disease

For as sure as powdered eggs is eggs
There'll be spam fritters still for tea
Morrissey dancing round his maypole
With Arthur Askey's busy bumblebee

We'll rise with pride like Victoria sponge
We'll bounce back like the bounciest castle
Pith helmets on, bang a gung-ho gong
We'll never, never be a vassal

We'll set sail in a golden pedalo
Bound for new colonies to conquer
We'll pay everyone in scratch cards
We'll sunbathe on the Costa Plonka

We'll spaff our talent all over the globe
We'll build a bridge to El Dorado
A bridge made from Great British irony
Quilted toilet rolls, pluck and bravado

Trousers round ankles, chasing empire's ghost
'Til death us do part, going, going, gone
Living a dream as the Benny Hill theme
Plays on and on and on and on and on

---

* A trip through the sunny uplands of deluded 'Boys' Own' British
exceptionalism via Brexit and 'herd immunity'. I started writing this piece
in the good old days BC (Before COVID-19), finishing it after coronavirus
had reached these shores. It seems to me that the myth of British (or
rather English) exceptionalism is itself a disease that has infected this
country. There doesn't appear to be any prospect of a vaccine. But there
is a video out there for this piece with music by DJ Mescalito.

FOLLOW THE SCIENCE
(A PUBLIC SERVICE ANNOUNCEMENT BY THE UK GOVERNMENT)

Best read in a Mr Cholmondley-Warner voice. There's a video with another DJ Mescalito tune on YouTube for this one too.

Death is knocking at the door
Shake his hand, show defiance
Ignore his grim, whispering scythe
Wash your hands, follow the science

Change the science, don't lick doorknobs
Go out if you must, stay at home
Lock it down and ramp it up
Paint a rainbow monochrome

Watch out! There's a mugger about!
Be unsure of a big surprise
Wrestle that mugger to the floor
He's invisible, use your eyes

Fight the enemy tooth and nail
Send him packing, take control
Sit on his sombrero, squash him
Whack him like a plastic mole

Clap for nurses dressed in bin bags
Doctors wearing Marigolds
Dance a conga round a care home
Jog for Jesus, don't catch colds

Keep calm, carry on, panic
Keep your distance side by side
Come out from your alpine tunnel
Move a mountain, turn the tide

Disinfect yourself with common sense
Your country needs you back to work
Over the top with Typhoid Mary
Do or die, be more Dunkirk

Sacrifice your health, save our wealth
Salute the contradictory
Fill up our world-beating morgues
Dig your own grave for victory

Stay alert, stop, look, listen, think
Careful now, say oops upside your head
Comb a giraffe, sit on a cornflake
Ride a black swan, eat garlic bread

Let your leaders spread the blame
Bury your silly little head in the sand
Mind your tone as they mask the truth
And wash, wash, wash their bloody hands

WHO DO I THINK I AM?

Dominic Cummings apparently has a 'tapestry room' in his £1.6 million
Islington townhouse. That's not an original Georgian feature. It was built
as part of an extension designed by upmarket architects. What the fuck
is a tapestry room for? Is it just full of antique embroidered cloth or
does he have a handloom in there? Does he come home after a hard day of
dismantling the apparatus of the state and unwind by weaving a giant
arras of Otto von Bismarck? We don't know.

I'm the bad-ass spad fresh outta the box
My brain is bigger than Mr Spock's

I'm the rebel renegade mastermind
Extra Special like Asda, one of a kind

I don't wanna brag, I don't wanna boast
But check out my hoodie; I'm sex on toast

I'm the hip-hop hepcat technocrat
I'm Jesus Christ in a beanie hat

I never tuck my shirt into my jeans
I'm ahead of my time like Milton Keynes

I'm a Bond villain in a body warmer
Yeah, I'm as hot as chicken korma

Satan loves me 'cause I'm diabolical
I'm Rasputin with challenged follicles

I'm Machiavelli, I'm Svengali
I'm *An Angry Egg* by Salvador Dali

I'm intergalactic, iconoclastic
Uber-Cumberbatch, bro – yo fantastic

I'm the zookeeper for the Tory chimps
I got all the negatives, bring out the gimps

I'm your uncrowned king, I pull the strings
I'm a fly guy, you can't clip my wings

I'm above the law, you're beneath my scorn
Gonna park my think tank on your lawn

I'm the Mekon man with a pandemic plan
Gonna sweep the weak into the trashcan

Gotta get eugenic when push comes to shove
I'm Dr Strangelove's black leather glove

I lurk in the murk of your worst nightmare
Gonna smash the system like Robespierre

I'm the chaos monkey, play it funky
When I eat a KitKat it's gotta be chunky

I dig intelligence that's artificial
The judiciary's whack, they're prejudicial

They can't touch me; I do as I please
I get my kicks from Thucydides

My bitch is rich, she's aristocratic
I'm anti-elite, that's axiomatic

I can see the future, I can see through you
My spectacles are made by Mr Magoo

I'm a preacher for Nietzsche, I'm Superman
Ich fahre nach Durham Town auf der Autobahn

I get it done, I deliver the goods
I dance to Abba in the bluebell woods

Strap up, mo'fo's at the BBC
I'm the daddy, don't you dare diss me

They call me Classic Dom, not Classic Dick
So fuck you all, I'm a dangerous prick*

Head to the website/YouTube to watch a video I've made with DJ
Mescalito for this one as well. Goodness, haven't we been busy wee bees?

* The Poesy Police have pointed out that I referred to someone as a
prick in another poem in this collection, which they regard as a bit
lackadaisical on my part. Other words that I seem to have an unconscious
affection for, as they appear more than once, include 'sticky-fingered',
'derrière', 'philistine', 'milk and honey', 'flighty', 'codpiece', 'spaff',
'pestilence', 'potentate', 'El Dorado' and 'Dunkirk'. Slightly disturbing when
you see them all together like this. By way of atonement, let's see if I
can write a verse that features them all and makes sense.

SUB-PRIME PESTILENCE

Sticky-fingered codpiece philistine pricks
Spaffed Blighty's milk and honey God knows where
Now their El Dorado is our Dunkirk
Their potentates' gold stashed up their derrieres*

> * There you go: a comprehensive analysis of the 2008 financial crisis in
> four lines. Well done me.

COVID'S METAMORPHOSES*

Life is shrink-wrapped, sanitised, sedated
Time is melting like unctuous Camembert
This is *Groundhog Day* by JG Ballard
Throbbing Gristle singing Sonny & Cher

* Pretentious pun alert.

WHAT DID YOU DO IN THE PLAGUE, DADDY?

Lockdown was strangely liberating to begin with. All pressure to be productive was removed. However, it didn't take long to start feeling inadequate.

I did not bake sourdough bread.

I did not learn Greek or read *Bleak House*.

I did not feel the burn doing 'bouncing bunnies' with Joe 'The Body Coach' Wicks.

I did not sing Bobby McFerrin's 1988 hit 'Don't Worry, Be Happy' in an a cappella Zoom choir.

I did not crochet my own crockery while watching Kirstie Allsopp's *Keep Crafting and Carry On*.

I did not clear out the under-stairs cupboard or the Augean stables.

I did not bake banana bread #nomnom.

I did not take up calligraphy.

I did not tattoo a rainbow on my forehead.

I did not Zumba in the street.

I did not put on a puppet show of Marcel Proust's *À la recherche du temps perdu*.

I did not play bebop jazz on my mediaeval crumhorn.

I did not increase my emotional bandwidth.

I did not knit Greek sourdough bread.

I did not livestream myself Riverdancing with a sourdough baguette stuck up my arse in front of my beautiful bookshelf crammed with important contemporary literature secretly chosen for the colour of the books' spines which when arranged alphabetically form an exact reproduction of a Mondrian painting.

I did not embark on a journey of self-discovery to unmap my life and acquire the tools to optimise my spiritual development, sharing my enhanced consciousness with the world by talking in an upward inflection.

I did not podcast.

I drank gin in the garden. In my pyjamas. With the cats.*

* I'm not sure why I bought a bottle of gin. I only ever drink it on a plane when we're going on holiday. Or at Gerve and Angela's house. It's got a funny reputation, gin. Used to be 'mother's ruin', now it's a hipster drink. To better understand the appeal of this intoxicating beverage I recommend a viewing of Gilbert and George's 1972 short film 'Gordon's Makes Us Drunk' - although I prefer Tanqueray, which is what I bought. Anyway, with all work cancelled for the foreseeable future (apart from my unremunerated job as a 24/7 cat butler) I gradually ramped up my consumption of said export-strength gin. Thus emboldened, I decided to launch a plea for financial assistance via what I believe is known as 'social media', as follows:
'Hi fans - I know you appreciate my work and think I'm a genius. Also I have nice ears. This May I was going to write a bestseller and then go on a book tour and then have it made into a film which I was going to star in and then I was going to buy the world. Obviously I can't do that now as I am shut in a house with two elderly cats and a dwindling supply of gin whilst my wife is away, incarcerated with her screaming, flatulent mother. Please send me all your money to show your appreciation of my talent and to allow me to go and live on a Greek island where I will think about what I want to write in my next life. I can send you a crap postcard with some smudged lipstick on it. Please log on to my JustSponging page and donate all you have as I'm sure you don't need any money during this crisis - you can't go out anywhere or on holiday. Thank you darlings. Mwahaha mwahaha xxx'
That should do the trick, I thought as I waited for the money to roll in. And waited. And waited. And waited.
However, I did receive help from the Arts Council's emergency funding. Hurrah! The cats will eat! Although they have started looking at their bowls in disgust, having decided that the flavour of the stockpiled special-offer gourmet mini fillets in jelly is not to their liking.

AN UNPRECEDENTED YEAR

2020. A year in which the use of the word 'unprecedented' has become unprecedented.

I've been keeping a diary. Defoe. Pepys. McGonagall. The chroniclers of mass distemper and infection provide a vital service, sending a 'message in a bottle' to future generations. If there are any. Unfortunately, most of this diary is illegible and covered in wine stains. The following entries have been salvaged.

25th January: Chinese New Year. New virus.

30th January: Feels like there's something coming in the air. And not in a Phil Collinsy kinda way. Even worse. An international public health emergency kinda way.

3rd March: Fresh from another holiday and undeterred by any newfangled disease, Britain's part-time Prime Minister and King of the World, Sir Borrissey-Boris de Spaffle Johnson, says that the UK is 'ready to take off its Clark Kent spectacles and leap into the phone booth, emerging with its cloak flowing as a supercharged champion'. Goodness. How terribly exciting.

11th March: Death tolls mounting in China and Italy. Pandemic declared. Bit of a worry.

12th March: Most of Europe starts shutting up shop, but In Britain it's 'business as usual', although some pensioners may have to die – #sadly.

13th March: The Cheltenham Gold Cup is won by a lively filly called 'Spread the Contagion'.

23rd March: Part-time PM Dolores Borissette says we must all stay at home but keep shaking hands. Hang on. No. Don't shake hands. Do that funny elbow thing.

29th March: Our bedroom curtain rail collapses.

2nd April: Good financial news. I receive £1.52 in royalties from an episode of *Taggart* I was in that was filmed over twenty years ago. Who needs Rishi Sunak? I was crushed to death with a barbell in my own gym, since you ask.

3rd April: I repair the curtain rail. Feel manly.

4th April: The government's world-leading chief medical officer Dr Hook says that if you have a beautiful body you should NOT hold it against him. Stand two metres away.*

7th April: Part-time PM Borisov Borisenko is in hospital with the virus. He's reported to be 'in good spirits at death's door'.

12th April: Easter Day. The Boris leaves hospital. Hallelujah. He hath arisen.

17th April: The Health Secretary Mr Handycock reveals that he does not have a magic wand but he's taking the right decisions at the right time and, after straining every sinew and leaving no stone unturned in a mammoth, Herculean effort to replenish his stock of empty platitudes, he's found a box of 'Tufty' badges in his sock drawer. Everybody clap now.

20th April: The endless roll call of heartbreaking deaths continues.

21st April: I strain every sinew and leave no stone unturned in a mammoth, Herculean effort to tidy the kitchen shelves. Find a tin of haggis – 'best before the end of October 2013' – an expiry date that's more recent than the government's PPE supplies. Do I dare eat it? I vow to take the right decision at the tight time.

23rd April: US President Dick Van Chucklefuck suggests sticking a torch up your arse and injecting yourself with Toilet Duck to combat the 'China virus'. Ah well. At least he didn't call it 'Italian pox'.

5th May: The official UK death toll is now 32,313, the worst in Europe. The true figure is likely to be over 55,000, although foreign secretary Dominic Raaaaab! says 'there are different ways of counting death'. Interesting news for undertakers.

8th May: Breaking news: Brian May hospitalised after tearing buttock muscles while gardening.

15th May: The government's world-leading chief medical officer Dr Feelgood says that drinking milk and alcohol might give us all immunity to coronavirus.

22nd May: Dear Respected Supreme Leader Kim Jong-un Cummings has been spotted driving blindfold to Durham Town because he's a huge Roger Whittaker fan. Perfectly reasonable. Nothing to see here. Move along now.

26th May: I paint the washing line poles a fetching shade of Colony Room green. Nice.

29th May: Still no updates on Brian May's buttocks.

2nd June: The 'alert level is transitioning'. Beam me up, Scotty. Lockdown is being relaxed. Despite posing no threat to social distancing, poetry gigs aren't mentioned. Disappointing.

8th June: I'm lying in a hammock on a Greek island beach with a cold beer, listening to reggae playing at the Kantina. I wish. Oh, how I wish.

20th June: The virus has mutated. US President and Big Orange Death Balloon Ronald McFlurry says it's now 'Kung-Flu'.

28th June: A breakthrough. The government's world-leading chief scientific advisor Dr Bunsen Honeydew is 'tickled pink' to announce the launch of his Virus Zapper.

24th July: 'Face coverings' become mandatory in England's shops. Captain Fray Bentos of the Royal Anti-Mask Fusiliers is unhappy. 'I didn't read *Boys' Own* comic book stories about two world wars to give in to Johnny Foreigner's germs,' he fumes. 'I will not relinquish an Englishman's inviolable right to catch and spread a deadly disease.'

25th July: Drinks Cabinet Secretary Grant Schnapps has flown to Spain by mistake.

27th July: Part-time, oven-ready Pieminister Lord Bunter of Borrisons urges everyone to eat half-price burgers for Britain. Drink tequila slammers. You fat bastards need to lose some weight. Let's do this!

30th July: The official UK death toll is now 45,999, including over 500 NHS and care workers. Part-time PM Jabberwock Johnson comes whiffling through the tulgey wood and burbles that the country has had 'a massive success in reducing the numbers of deaths'. Unusual use of the word 'success'.

31st July: Part-time PM Bertie Blusterwank says the UK must squeeze that brake pedal to bounce forward. It'll all be over by Christmas.**

17th August: The part-time PM is missing.

18th August: The part-time PM has been tracked and traced and is found hiding in a tent in the Scottish highlands dressed in nothing but a high-vis jacket and hard hat, shouting, 'Aedificate! Aedificate! Aedificate!'

27th August: The official UK death toll is now 41,477, which is 4,522 less than on 30th July. More interesting news for undertakers. Indeed, a 'massive success'.

world class

* Mr Peter Ward of Stockport has pointed out that it was The Bellamy Brothers who sang "If I Said You Had A Beautiful Body Would You Hold It Against Me?". Not Dr Hook. Whoops. I've confused my double entendre, innuendo laden pop songs. Dr Hook sang "When You're In Love With A Beautiful Woman It Gets Hard". Mea culpa.

** It won't, will it? I've been helping shield my ninety-one- year-old in-laws since March so the new Lockdown 2 is really just the ninth month of Lockdown 1 for me. The only difference being that instead of gin in the garden in my pyjamas with the cats it's now red wine on the sofa in my pyjamas with the cats watching box-sets of Nordic noir. They're particularly fond of 'The Bridge'. Anyway, I fully expect to emerge blinking into the sunshine in about thirty years' time, like a Japanese soldier leaving the jungle decades after the end of World War II.

HELP YOURSELF
(ANOTHER PUBLIC SERVICE ANNOUNCEMENT BY THE UK GOVERNMENT)

Fight germs in the airport lounge
Fight germs on foreign beaches
Fight your fears, sweat blood and tears
Recycle Churchill speeches

Keep Mammon alive 9 to 5
Commute for the greater glory
Dulce et decorum est
Pro Pret a Manger mori

Eat out to spread it about
Drop Jägerbombs on the virus
U-turn, reverse your ferret
Twerk from home with Miley Cyrus

Heed the rule of six feet under
Comply with the *Da Vinci Code*
Hands, face, space, drink, feck, arse
Follow the yellow brick road

Save Christmas, never surrender
Don't let the bells end, don't give in
Get roaring drunk by 10pm
Let your hair down with discipline

Stiffen sinews, do your duty
England expects you to behave
Lock all empty stable doors
Wear smiley masks at a rave

Book a Covid test in Narnia
Isolate together without fail
Download Aladdin's magic app
Track and trace the Holy Grail

Load up with silver bullets
Aim high, shoot grouse on the moon
Button up your overcoat
Whistle a happy tune

Don't look back in anger
Don't take your love to town
Hold a chicken in the air
Do the disco duck, get down

Help yourself, be viable
Find a new job, do the right thing
Cross your fingers, clutch at straws
Hibernate, wake up next spring

THE THUNDER MUTTERS
(AFTER JOHN CLARE*)

The thunder mutters louder, louder yet
Long stifled voices choked of breath resound
Icons of wealth wrung from African sweat
Cut down like sugar cane fall to the ground**
Good trouble surges, hope rises unbound
Belief iron-fisted fear cannot scatter
Stop and search your soul, prejudice confound
Call it out, let the white silence shatter
The thunder rends the skies – black lives matter

* Written for the poet Adam Horovitz's podcast of the same name and in
the form of the original John Clare poem – i.e. a 'Spenserian stanza' (nine
lines rhymed ababbcbcc), as used by Edmund Spenser in his unfinished
epic poem 'The Faerie Queene'. Waits for round of applause. Not a sausage.

** Cheerio Mr Colston and good riddance.

MOLOTOV COCKTAIL HOUR

Lyrics for a new Resurrectors' song. Altogether now, 'Sous les pavés, la plage!'

Snake oil spivs are running the show
Narcissus is top of the bill
Educated fools born to rule
Cartoon fascist vaudeville

They're telling you that blood is blue
They say hey our pigs can fly
They're selling ground unicorn horn
They're feeding you pie in the sky

No time now for protest songs
No time for flower power
Uncork the booze, light the fuse
It's Molotov cocktail hour

They're pointing at the scapegoats
They're hoisting a partisan rag
They're looting your tomorrows
They're trousering the swag

They're tossing you their stale crumbs
They cut the cake, you pay the price
Heads they win, tails you lose
They're rolling loaded dice

No time now for protest songs
No time for flower power
Uncork the booze, light the fuse
It's Molotov cocktail hour

They're burning all your bridges
They're keeping you in your place
They're snorting in their golden trough
They're laughing in your face

Tired of touch the forelock
Cap in hand on bended knee
Tired of kowtow, bow and scrape
Please wipe your boots on me

No time now for protest songs
No time for flower power
Uncork the booze, light the fuse
It's Molotov cocktail hour

No more beg, lie down, roll over
No more three-bags-full-sir sheep
No more creeping Jesus
No more Uriah Heep

No more grin and bear it
No more swallow the pill
No more knuckle under
No more grist to the mill

No time now for protest songs
No time for flower power
Uncork the booze, light the fuse
It's Molotov cocktail hour

No more robes of ermine
No more powdered periwigs
No more bejewelled monarchs
No more gilded Mr Bigs

No more pomp and circumstance
No more the tinsel show
No more old school tie old boy
No more their status quo

No time now for protest songs
No time for flower power
Uncork the booze, light the fuse
*It's Molotov cocktail hour**

* This piece was born out of anger, frustration and despondency about
the state of the world and its lurch to far right populism. However, the
US election results have provided a glimmer of optimism so let's try and
finish on a positive note with this next one.

ALCHEMY

Disaster, despair, desolation, fear
The daily shock and horror hue and cry
Yet in a corner of this weary world
There's a man making diamonds from the sky*

There's a footballer feeding the hungry
There's an artist saving souls lost at sea
There are strangers pulling lives from ruin
Untold tenderness shows who we can be

Selfless compassion turns rust into gold
It un-cages our hope and lets it fly
For we are the stuff of stardust and dreams
And we can all make diamonds from the sky

* Ecotricity founder Dale Vince is planning to make diamonds from
carbon, water and energy sourced directly from the elements at a "sky
mining" facility in Stroud.

What next? Who knows? All we can do is take heed of the sage advice given to Bertie Wooster by Jeeves, that whatever ordeal lies ahead "there are always cocktails".

"Where Manchester has John Cooper Clarke, Dundee has Elvis McGonagall. Wonderful writing, tack-sharp humour and uncompromising politics. Hilarious." (Marissa Burgess, The List)

"A stream of beautifully worded invective....brilliant wit and wordplay." (David Chadderton, British Theatre Guide)

"Pin-pointed satires, dynamic performances and meticulous impressions. Electrifying, bitingly funny and politically astute." (Michael Horovitz)

"McGonaglls? Deadbeat poet." (Mr Szczypkowski, janitor and proprietor of the Promised Land Inconvenience Store at the Graceland Caravan Park)

"In all my years as a celebrity hairdresser, I can honestly say I have never seen anything like it! 10 out of 10 for nerve but book an appointment soon!" (Dexter Clark, London, New York, Paris, Broughty Ferry)

"Someone you've never heard of whose every stanza sounds like it was written by Les Dawson on the back of a fag packet." (Rachel Cooke, The New Statesman)

"I've been on Radio 4 more recently than him you know." (Charlie McGonagall, feline-in-residence at The Graceland Caravan Park and featured artiste on Broadcasting House)

"More poems? Whatever. I can do a really good yowl that sounds like Kenneth Williams." (Jasper McGonagall, also feline-in-residence at the Graceland Caravan Park)

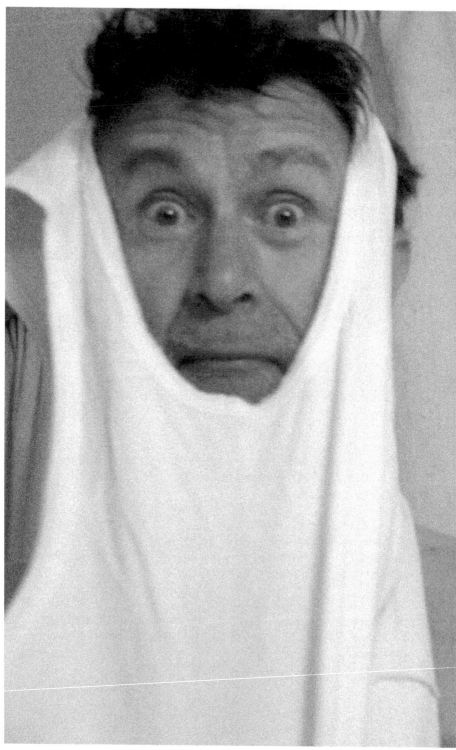

Lockdown.

THANKS AND ACKNOWLEDGEMENTS

Thanks to Clive Birnie, Bridget Hart, Harriet Evans and everyone at Burning Eye Books.

To Tony Kerins for the illustrations.

To Andrew Lee for the cover photo: @PhotographyAndrewLee

To Si, Seb and all The Resurrectors for the music.

To Derek O'Sullivan for digital beats and eye-candy visuals.

To Michelle Abadie for new website design:
http://www.abadie.co.uk/

To Miles Warde for the *Archive on 4* commissions.

To Frank Stirling at 7digital for tying the room together.

To the Laura Kinsella Foundation for sponsoring my 2018 Edinburgh show, *Full Tartan Jacket* and to Simon, Liz, Lily, Laura and Mia at Braunholtz Mansions and Bex Colwell at unavoidable pr for looking after me during that Edinburgh run.

To Mr Poon Kee, Hong Kong tailor, for a fine tartan dinner jacket - now technically "vintage".

To The Prince Albert in Stroud for being fabulous.

To all my mates on the stand-up poetry circuit and all the tireless promoters who've booked me for gigs.

To Kit Braunholtz for a vat of lockdown wine.

And to Helen for everything.

www.elvismcgonagall.co.uk

Milton Keynes UK
Ingram Content Group UK Ltd.
UKHW011842010823
426160UK00002B/15

9 781911 570950